DIARY OF PRAYERS & SELF-ES
for the DAUGHTERS

Prayers
for
Daddy's
Girls

TATE PUBLISHING
AND ENTERPRISES, LLC

Published by Tate Publishing & Enterprises, LLC
127 E. Trade Center Terrace | Mustang, Oklahoma 73064 USA
1.888.361.9473 | www.tatepublishing.com

Tate Publishing is committed to excellence in the publishing industry. The company reflects the philosophy established by the founders, based on Psalm 68:11,
"The Lord gave the word and great was the company of those who published it."

Book design copyright © 2014 by Tate Publishing, LLC. All rights reserved.
Cover design by Junriel Boquecosa
Interior design by Honeylette Pino

Published in the United States of America

ISBN: 978-1-68028-090-6
1. Religion / Christian Life / Devotional
2. Religion / Christian Life / Inspirational
14.10.30

Acknowledgments

I WOULD LIKE TO honor and acknowledge my dear mother Belinda Walton-Henry for teaching me the importance of prayer. I thank you, Mother, for the sacrifices you made as a single parent raising three children. I know it was hard and painful at times, but God was the head of our house, and we made it through those tough times because of prayer and church. When I was younger, I couldn't understand why my sister and I had to attend church activities, prayer meetings, choir rehearsals, and Sunday service almost four times a week. But I now understand why you did it, and I am a better man because of your obedience to God. I salute you, Mother.

Contents

Introduction

THIS BOOK WAS specifically written for God's daughters who are hurting and dealing with low self-esteem and also for the unsaved daughters, the depressed, the sexually and physically abused daughters, the fatherless, the confused, the frustrated, the lost, the daughters suffering from a crushed self-esteem, and for the daughters of God who simply want to be loved. This book of prayer and affirmations was ordained, ochestrated, and written just for you.

Prayers for Daddy's Girls is a book of prayers, self-esteem affirmations, and personal journal entries which should be used as a guideline for you to rebuild your wounded self-esteem. You should read this book in addition to reading the Holy Scriptures, while also praying and meditating on God.

God had you in mind when he spoke these words to me. He gave me the wisdom, knowledge, and understanding needed to assist in healing your wounds and mending your broken hearts. I want every woman reading this book to know that you are God's special and precious daughter, and he loves and cares for each and every one of you. He hears your public cries and he sees your silent tears. As a man of God, I believe it is my duty to protect you, the precious women of God, by informing and equipping you with the most powerful weapon you have, which is the power of prayer.

As a man, I believe I am able to write a book of prayer for women, because I grew up watching my mother struggle as a single parent raising three children by herself. And as a young child, I was there to see the tears, the hurt, the pain that my mother was bearing. But even though she carried so many burdens and dealt with so many dissapointments, I always saw her lying on her face and crying out to God. There were so many times I felt her pain even when she didn't show it, but through it all, I would always see her praying. And since I was a child, my mother has constantly taught and reminded me to take everything to God in prayer. So you should also cast all your cares and burdens to your Father in heaven.

I recall going through my own personal trials and tribulations, and I was comforted in knowing that Jesus knows about my troubles, and he knows the story that lives inside of every tear drop. It is a wonderful feeling to know that God cares about you. And it is amazing to know that even when I don't feel love, I know he loves me unconditionally through all of my guilt, shame, pain, and dissapointments. I want you to imagine God extending his arms toward you, and now imagine him holding you tight as a Father embraces his daughter. And now imagine the release of tears and adoration that would flow from you while you are lying in your Father's arms. And as he holds you close to him, listen to him whisper softly in your ear, "Everything is going to be all right." It is a sweet and soothing feeling to lay in the arms of a loving God.

When I was a college student at The New School University in New York City, I took several psychology courses, and I recall reviewing a psychological study which proved that negative words spoken over a person can result in severe damage to one's self-esteem. For example, if a parent constantly tells their child or teenager, "You're dumb, you're stupid, you're just like you're father, you'll never amount to anything, you're so bad." Then that child will eventually enter into adulthood with those negative stigmas on their lives which will result in low-self esteem, risky behaviors, or other negative psychological problems.

But I firmly believe that by praying, having positive thinking, and reciting positive affirmations over your life, then you will gradually break free from the chains of negativity. Therefore, I have provided positive affirmations after each pray, and you should recite these affirmations over your life every single day until a positive change begins to happen. So I want you to pray to God every day, read God's word, and say these affirmations to yourself, and I believe you will begin to feel better about who you are as God begins to revive, restore, and rebuild your self-esteem.

I have also provided a journal after each prayer for you to write down your own personal prayers to God, and then following your personal prayers, there is a section where you can express your thanks to God as you begin to see progress. I received this revelation while doing some spring cleaning in 2012, and as I was cleaning, I came across a composition notebook which was almost twenty-five years old. This notebook was unique because it was my prayer and testimony notebook which was a requirement when I was in elementary school.

As a child, I attended a Christian School in Newark, New Jersey, and as part of the curriculum, the students were required to keep a weekly prayer journal which also included the current date of the prayer request. And then as God answered our prayer requests, we were required to write down this testimony along with the date. So as I began to open my old and worn prayer book, I started to look at some of my own personal prayer request during that time. And I saw a prayer entry I made in 1986 which read, "God, please help my dad to stop smoking," and the other prayer request was, "Lord, please save my dad." And when I turned the page to read my personal praise and testimonies section, I noticed that I made an entry in 1990 which read, "God, I thank you for helping my dad to stop smoking!"

So I decided to take that same concept and apply it to the daughters of God. I believe it is vital to not only pray, but it is vital to recognize and record when God answers your prayers. It is encouraging to look back over your life and to see what the mighty hand of God has done for you. For instance, beginning in 1986, I prayed for twenty years that God would save my dad's soul, and before my father passed away on December 6, 2006, I saw and witnessed God save my father's soul! And before he passed away, me and my dad would talk on the phone for hours about the word of God. My mother told me when I was younger that I would go up for prayer every Sunday and ask God to save my dad's soul.

And I am so overjoyed to tell you that my dad was saved, sanctified, and filled with Holy Spirit before he died. I am a living witness that God can and will answer prayers! God does answer prayers! And God is able to answer your prayers, he is able to make ways where there is no visible way, he is able to save your soul, and save the souls of your family members, he is able to heal you, he is able to comfort you, and he is able to perform miracles in your life. I have seen God do some wonderous things in my life, and I believe he will do the same for you too. So just keep the faith, keep praying, give all your problems to God, and watch God move in a mighty way for you! Be blessed, and be encouraged, precious daughters of God.

My Prayer for Women

DEAR GOD,

I ask that you help every woman that reads this book to receive complete and total healing and transformation. Please heal the wounds of their broken hearts and the wounds of their pasts. Bless them with your strength and guidance and restore their self-esteem so they know who they are as women of God. Lord, let these women have a better understanding and deeper relationship with you as a result of a stronger prayer life. I ask these things in your precious name, amen.

The Absent Father

Prayers

Dear God,

I ask that you heal me from the pain, the hurt, and the rejections of not having my own father in my life. I thank you for being my heavenly father, and I ask that you heal the wounds which were left behind by my biological father. God, please mend my broken heart, and I ask that you be the father that I never had. Please place positive male role models in my life to guide and mentor me. Lord, help me to smile again, show me how to be a woman of God, and help me to heal and move forward in confidence knowing that I am one of your daughters. "Keep me as the apple of the eye, and hide me under the shadow of thy wings" (Psalms 17:8, KJV). I ask these things in your mighty name, amen.

Daily Affirmations

1. I am not my father's mistakes.
2. I am one of God's precious daughters.
3. I will begin to love myself.
4. I will heal from the wounds of my father.
5. I will smile again.

Personal Prayers

Dear God:

_____

_____

_____

_____

Dear God:

_____

_____

_____

_____

Dear God:

_____

_____

_____

_____

Dear God:

_____

_____

_____

_____

Thank You Notes

Father, I thank you for:

_____

_____

_____

_____

Father, I thank you for:

_____

_____

_____

_____

Father, I thank you for:

_____

_____

_____

_____

Father, I thank you for:

_____

_____

_____

_____

My Self-Esteem

Prayers

Dear god,

I ask that you assist me in building and rebuilding my self-esteem so that I may know who I am as a person and as a woman of God. There have been many obstacles, challenges, and bad relationships in my life that have caused me to feel bad about myself. I am tired of feeling this way, and I want to be able to look in the mirror and like what I see. But at this moment, I have issues with having a low self-esteem. So, Father, please help me as I deal with the struggles of my own insecurities. Please heal the areas in my life that have caused me to become insecure and allow me to smile again. And, God, give me the strength to break free from anyone who contributes to my damaged self-esteem. God, thank you for loving me, and thank you for allowing me to feel good about myself, amen.

Daily Affirmations

1. I am a beautiful and attractive woman.
2. I am fearfully and wondefully made.
3. I love myself, and I love who I am.
4. I will not allow others to determine who I am.
5. I will look in the mirror and smile again.

Personal Prayers

Dear God:

_____

_____

_____

_____

Dear God:

_____

_____

_____

_____

Dear God:

_____

_____

_____

_____

Dear God:

_____

_____

_____

_____

Thank You Notes

Father, I thank you for:

_____

_____

_____

_____

Father, I thank you for:

_____

_____

_____

_____

Father I thank you for:

_____

_____

_____

_____

Father, I thank you for:

_____

_____

_____

_____

Abandonment

Prayers

Dear god,

I need your help in coping with these feelings of abandonment. There were times in my life when I was abandoned by my parents, other family member, a friend, loved ones, and I haven't seemed to recover from those hurtful feelings of being abandoned. So I need you to help me, and I need you to teach me through your word and through your wisdom the ways to get through this hurt and pain of being abandoned. I thank you in advance for my positive change, amen.

Daily Affirmations

1. I will heal from the scars of abandonment.

2. I will not let abandonment define who I am.

3. I thank God for never leaving me.

4. I will recover from this hurt and pain.

5. God will give me strength to move forward.

Personal Prayers

Dear God:

_____

_____

_____

_____

Dear God:

_____

_____

_____

_____

Dear God:

_____

_____

_____

_____

Dear God:

_____

_____

_____

_____

Thank You Notes

Father, I thank you for:

_____

_____

_____

_____

Father, I thank you for:

_____

_____

_____

_____

Father, I thank you for:

_____

_____

_____

_____

Father, I thank you for:

_____

_____

_____

_____

Love and Acceptance

TYRIS ELIJAH HENRY III

Dᴇᴀʀ ɢᴏᴅ,

There are times when I don't feel loved, and there are many times when I desperately want to be accepted by others. But I don't want to receive this love and acceptance from the wrong people. I have heard so many times how much God loves me, but at this very moment, I really need to feel your love. So, God, I stretch my hands to thee, and I ask that you stretch your hands toward me, and hold me in your arms as a father embraces his daughter. I thank you, Father, for showering me with your unconditional and everlasting love. And I thank you for accepting me as one of your own daughters. Thank you for loving me, amen!

Daily Affirmations

1. God loves me so much.
2. God accepts me when no one else does.
3. I am learning to love myself.
4. I accept myself.
5. I choose to love and be loved.

Personal Prayers

Dear God:

_____

_____

_____

_____

Dear God:

_____

_____

_____

_____

Dear God:

_____

_____

_____

_____

Dear God:

_____

_____

_____

_____

Thank You Notes

Father, I thank you for:

_____

_____

_____

_____

Father, I thank you for:

_____

_____

_____

_____

Father, I thank you for:

_____

_____

_____

_____

Father, I thank you for:

_____

_____

_____

_____

Filling the Void

Prayers

D EAR GOD,

I come before you knowing that I have empty spaces in my life, and I'm asking you to fill those voids with your Holy Spirit. I'm concerned that I might fill those voids with people and things that aren't good for me, so I want you to come into my life and occupy the empty space within me. Please protect me from negative influences and free me and deliver me from the negativity which I've allowed to enter into my life. I ask that you fill my empty space with your love, your joy, and your peace. I say yes to your will for my life, and I welcome your sweet spirit to fill every void in my life, amen.

Daily Affirmations

1. God will fill the empty areas of my life.
2. I will guard myself from negative influences.
3. I will fill the voids by reading God's word.
4. I will fill the voids by meditating and praying.
5. I speak love, joy, peace, and happiness in my life.

Personal Prayers

Dear God:

_____

_____

_____

_____

Dear God:

_____

_____

_____

_____

Dear God:

_____

_____

_____

_____

Dear God:

_____

_____

_____

_____

Thank You Notes

Father, I thank you for:

_____

_____

_____

_____

Father, I thank you for:

_____

_____

_____

_____

Father, I thank you for:

_____

_____

_____

_____

Father, I thank you for:

_____

_____

_____

_____

Anger and Frustration

Prayers

Dear God,

There are so many challenges that have occurred in my past that have caused me to become so angry and frustrated. I have been told by so many people that I have to free myself from this anger, but, God, I don't know how to let it go, and I need your help. I am angry about things from my childhood, angry about past decisions, and frustrated about failed relationships. In addition, I even realized that I am dealing with anger from past issues with my own parents. But today, I want to forgive and free myself from this anger. God, please help me to properly deal with situations that cause me to become angry and frustrated. I want to do better, and I thank you for helping me. Amen.

Daily Affirmations

1. I will stop and remain calm when I am frustrated.

2. I will use self-control when I am angry.

3. I will not allow anger to rule over my life.

4. God is helping me deal with the root of my anger.

5. I have decided to free myself from anger, frustration, and bitterness.

Personal Prayers

Dear God:

_____

_____

_____

_____

Dear God:

_____

_____

_____

_____

Dear God:

_____

_____

_____

_____

Dear God:

_____

_____

_____

_____

Thank You Notes

Father, I thank you for:

_____

_____

_____

_____

Father, I thank you for:

_____

_____

_____

_____

Father, I thank you for:

_____

_____

_____

_____

Father, I thank you for:

_____

_____

_____

_____

Dating a Godly Man

Prayers

DEAR GOD,

I ask that you prepare me for the godly man that you have especially for me. And as you prepare me, I ask that you do a new thing in me and build me up so that I am the godly woman that he is also seeking. Father, wherever he is in this world, I ask that you protect him, mold him, and make him into the man that you would have him to be. And I ask that you bring us together during your appointed time. I thank you in advance for sending me this Godly man who will be my friend, my helper, and eventually my husband. Amen.

Daily Affirmations

1. God has someone special just for me.
2. I will pray and seek God when dating.
3. I will ask God to prepare me for marriage.
4. I will not be unequally yoked while in a relationhip.
5. I will only be treated with love and respect.

Personal Prayers

Dear God:

_____

_____

_____

_____

Dear God:

_____

_____

_____

_____

Dear God:

_____

_____

_____

_____

Dear God:

_____

_____

_____

_____

Thank You Notes

Father, I thank you for:

_____

_____

_____

_____

Father, I thank you for:

_____

_____

_____

_____

Father, I thank you for:

_____

_____

_____

_____

Father, I thank you for:

_____

_____

_____

_____

Feeling Vulnerable

Prayers

Dear god,

I feel so emotional and vulnerable right now, and I need you to teach me how to control my emotions. I ask that you strengthen me and guide me through those days when I am feeling vulnerable. I know that the enemy is watching and studying me, especially during those periods of my vulnerability. During these times, please protect me from my own wants and desires which may cause me to sin against you. I ask that you place your whole armor of protection over me, so I may withstand the temptations of the enemy. I ask these things in your precious name, amen.

Daily Affirmations

1. I will remain strong when I am vulnerable.
2. I will pray during my vulnerable times.
3. God will protect me from harm when I am vulnerable.
4. I am strong and not weak.
5. God will help me control my emotions.

Personal Prayers

Dear God:

_____

_____

_____

_____

Dear God:

_____

_____

_____

_____

Dear God:

_____

_____

_____

_____

Dear God:

_____

_____

_____

_____

Thank You Notes

Father, I thank you for:

_____

_____

_____

_____

Father, I thank you for:

_____

_____

_____

_____

Father, I thank you for:

_____

_____

_____

_____

Father, I thank you for:

_____

_____

_____

_____

Dealing with Lust

Prayers

DEAR GOD,

I ask that you please take control of my thoughts and my emotions as I am bombarded with sexual images and lustful desires. Lord, you created me, so you must know what I'm feeling right now. Father, sometimes, it seems so hard to resist the temptations of lust, especially during those late nights when I'm all alone and feeling lonely. But here I am, Lord, praying to you in the midnight hour as I'm struggling and wrestling with lust. I need your help, Lord. Please strengthen me so that I may resist these lustful desires that are burning from within me. Father, please lead and guide me so that I may make the right decision at this very moment. I don't want to slip, and I don't want to fall. So, God, I ask that you help me. And for the times that I have failed and answered the calls of lust, Father, I ask that you forgive me and give me another chance. I thank you for helping me, and thank you for your grace and mercy! Amen.

Daily Affirmations

1. I will pray right away when faced with lust.

2. I will ask God to send a strong prayer partner.

3. I will call my prayer partner for support.

4. I will abstain from pornography and other sexual images.

5. I will continue to pray for strength against lust.

Personal Prayers

Dear God:

_____

_____

_____

_____

Dear God:

_____

_____

_____

_____

Dear God:

_____

_____

_____

_____

Dear God:

_____

_____

_____

_____

Thank You Notes

Father, I thank you for:

_____

_____

_____

_____

Father, I thank you for:

_____

_____

_____

_____

Father, I thank you for:

_____

_____

_____

_____

Father, I thank you for:

_____

_____

_____

_____

Coping with Divorce

Prayers

DEAR GOD,

Since I have gone through this divorce, I have had feelings of being depressed, lonely, afraid, rejected, confused, angry, and even guilty. My current feelings have been an emotional roller coaster, and I desperately need your assistance in coping with these feelings of despair. I want to get through this, I want to move forward, I want to heal from this divorce, but I really need your help. I ask that you hold my hand through this process and prepare me for any future relationships. I believe I will recover from this divorce. Thank you, Lord. Amen.

Daily Affirmations

1. I will allow myself to heal from this divorce.

2. I will choose to move forward.

3. I will not self-medicate by using drugs, alcohol, or other risky behaviors.

4. I will keep a journal of my feelings and progress.

5. I will attend divorce counseling or support groups.

Personal Prayers

Dear God:

_____

_____

_____

_____

Dear God:

_____

_____

_____

_____

Dear God:

_____

_____

_____

_____

Dear God:

_____

_____

_____

_____

Thank You Notes

Father, I thank you for:

_____

_____

_____

_____

Father, I thank you for:

_____

_____

_____

_____

Father, I thank you for:

_____

_____

_____

_____

Father, I thank you for:

_____

_____

_____

_____

The Single Mother

Prayers

DEAR GOD,

I believe that you see and understand the struggles I am facing as a single mother. I know that I can do all things through Christ, but sometimes, I get so exhausted and frustrated raising a child by myself. I am trying very hard to provide financially, emotionally, and spiritually to my child, but I feel as though I can't do this alone. God, I need your help. Your Holy Word says that you will never leave me nor forsake me. Please give me the strength I need to raise my children to become wise men and women of God. As my heavenly father, I ask you to provide food, clothing, and shelter for me and my children. And I also ask you to place a strong and positive male role model in their lives. Thank you for you help. Amen.

Daily Affirmations

1. I am a good mother.
2. I am a strong woman of God.
3. My children will be successful in life.
4. God will provide for me and my children.
5. God loves me, and he did not forget about me.

Personal Prayers

Dear God:

_____

_____

_____

_____

Dear God:

_____

_____

_____

_____

Dear God:

_____

_____

_____

_____

Dear God:

_____

_____

_____

_____

Thank You Notes

Father, I thank you for:

Father, I thank you for:

Father, I thank you for:

Father, I thank you for:

Saving My Marriage

Prayers

D<small>EAR GOD,</small>

I am trying so hard to save my marriage, but it seems like things just aren't working out. I admit that things aren't going well now, but my husband and I have had some great times in our marriage, and I believe what we have is worth saving. I do not want to walk away without trying everything in my power to save this marriage. I ask you to rebuke any attacks that the enemy has planned against my marriage. So I need your wisdom and guidance and your divine intervention as my husband and I try to reconcile our marriage. Lord, you know what's best for me, so please lead me and direct me in the right direction. Amen.

Daily Affirmations

1. I will seek marriage counseling and Godly advice.
2. The plans of the enemy will not destroy this marriage.
3. I will seek God and communicate with my husband.
4. I will meditate on the good times in my marriage.
5. I will honor God by honoring my wedding vows.

Personal Prayers

Dear God:

_____

_____

_____

_____

Dear God:

_____

_____

_____

_____

Dear God:

_____

_____

_____

_____

Dear God:

_____

_____

_____

_____

Thank You Notes

Father, I thank you for:

_____

_____

_____

_____

Father, I thank you for:

_____

_____

_____

_____

Father, I thank you for:

_____

_____

_____

_____

Father, I thank you for:

_____

_____

_____

_____

Guilt and Shame

Prayers

Dᴇᴀʀ ɢᴏᴅ,

I have done some things, and I have gone through some things that may not have been pleasing in your eyes. And these things that have been done in secret now cause me to have feelings of guilt and shame about myself, and I don't want to feel this way anymore. God, forgive me for my sins and forgive me for the wrong things I've done that have dissapointed you. So today, I ask you to wash guilt and shame from me and allow me to walk with my head held high, knowing that I am free from the guilty stains. In your name I pray, amen.

Daily Affirmations

1. I am free from the guilt of my past.

2. Shame has been washed away from me.

3. I am redeemed by the Blood of Christ.

4. I will not allow others to remind me of past sins.

5. I will experience happiness once again.

Personal Prayers

Dear God:

_____

_____

_____

_____

Dear God:

_____

_____

_____

_____

Dear God:

_____

_____

_____

_____

Dear God:

_____

_____

_____

_____

Thank You Notes

Father, I thank you for:

_____

_____

_____

_____

Father, I thank you for:

_____

_____

_____

_____

Father, I thank you for:

_____

_____

_____

_____

Father, I thank you for:

_____

_____

_____

_____

My Broken Heart

Prayers

DEAR GOD,

My heart has been broken from past relationships, a recent break-up, and other complicated issues. It is difficult for me to explain the pain and sadness I feel inside. I don't even know the words to describe what I'm feeling, but I am simply asking you to just heal and mend my broken heart.

Daily Affirmations

1. I have the strength to move forward.
2. I deserve to be happy.
3. I will not allow my past to determine my future.
4. I will heal from this broken heart.
5. God is the potter, and he will fix my wounded heart.

Prayers

Dear God:

_____

_____

_____

_____

Dear God:

_____

_____

_____

_____

Dear God:

_____

_____

_____

_____

Dear God:

_____

_____

_____

_____

Thank You Notes

Father, I thank you for:

_____

_____

_____

_____

Father, I thank you for:

_____

_____

_____

_____

Father, I thank you for:

_____

_____

_____

_____

Father, I thank you for:

_____

_____

_____

_____

Feeling Depressed

Prayers

DEAR GOD,

I come before you asking that you relieve me from this spirit of depression. Lord, I feel like there's so much weight on me at times. And it seems like I can't take any more punches. I feel like if I'm faced with one more obstacle, then I won't be able to make it through the day. Lord, I ask that you please help me! Bless me with the wisdom and strength to overcome this depressive state of mind. God, help me to step out of my dark cave, and give me the willpower to let go of the things and situations that have me mentally bound. Father, I feel so tired, and I can't do this on my own. I need your help in order to make it through. I cry out to you to lift the heavy burdens from my life. At this moment, I ask that you touch me and place a robe of joy, peace, and gladness over my shoulders. I thank you, Father, for renewing me and for bringing me out of depression. Amen.

Daily Affirmations

1. The obstacles in my life will not overpower me.

2. God will give me the strength to step out of this depression.

3. The test and trials in my life are only temporary.

4. I will not give up! I will win!

5. I will seek professional or pastorial counseling if needed.

Personal Prayers

Dear God:

_____

_____

_____

_____

Dear God:

_____

_____

_____

_____

Dear God:

_____

_____

_____

_____

Dear God:

_____

_____

_____

_____

Thank You Notes

Father, I thank you for:

_____

_____

_____

_____

Father, I thank you for:

_____

_____

_____

_____

Father, I thank you for:

_____

_____

_____

_____

Father, I thank you for:

_____

_____

_____

_____

Loneliness

Prayers

Dear god,

There are times when I feel so lonely. Even though I know that I am not alone, I still have moments of loneliness. During these lonely times, I wonder what Your Son Jesus did when he was all alone. And then I heard someone say, Jesus prayed during these times. So I come to you asking you to help me in this state of loneliness. I ask that you fill that void and emptiness in me that may be causing me to feel lonely. Lord, please send a traveler every now and then to help me and encourage me during this journey. God, I know that you will never leave me nor forsake me. I thank you, Lord, for loving me and for being there for me. I know that as long as you are with me, I will never be alone. Amen.

Daily Affirmations

1. God will not leave me or forsake me.

2. God will feel the voids of loneliness in my life.

3. God will comfort me during those times when I feel lonely.

4. God will send help to assist me during these times of loneliness.

5. God will be there for me even when no one else is around.

Personal Prayers

Dear God:

_____

_____

_____

_____

Dear God:

_____

_____

_____

_____

Dear God:

_____

_____

_____

_____

Dear God:

_____

_____

_____

_____

Thank You Notes

Father, I thank you for:

_____

_____

_____

_____

Father, I thank you for:

_____

_____

_____

_____

Father, I thank you for:

_____

_____

_____

_____

Father, I thank you for:

_____

_____

_____

_____

Dealing with Rejection

Prayers

D EAR GOD,

There have been so many times in my life when I was rejected by family, friends, or in a relationship, and I'm coming to you today to ask that you heal the wounds of the rejected and hurt little girl who lives within me. As a child, I dealt with rejection, and I didn't realize how being rejected played a huge role in who I am as a woman. I also ask you to heal me from the pain of being rejected from own father. But today, I ask that you take that pain away, and I ask you take away the fear of any future rejection. I also ask that you protect me from repeating the cycle of rejection in my children's lives. I thank you by faith for healing me from rejection. In your mighty name I pray, amen.

Daily Affirmations

1. I will strive to forgive those who rejected me.

2. I will overcome the fear of rejection.

3. I know God will never reject me.

4. I will not live life being afraid of getting rejected.

5. God loves and cares for me.

Personal Prayers

Dear God:

_____

_____

_____

_____

Dear God:

_____

_____

_____

_____

Dear God:

_____

_____

_____

_____

Dear God:

_____

_____

_____

_____

Thank You Notes

Father, I thank you for:

_____

_____

_____

_____

Father, I thank you for:

_____

_____

_____

_____

Father, I thank you for:

_____

_____

_____

_____

Father, I thank you for:

_____

_____

_____

_____

Don't Compromise

Prayers

DEAR GOD,

I don't want to compromise or give into the temptations of this world. Please help me not to compromise and settle for less in my relationships, my career, or in my life. I ask that you give me boldness and strength to stand out when others are compromising, and conforming to this world. Forgive me for taking for granting the gifts, the talents, and the anointing that you've placed on my life. I ask that you place your hedge of protection over me. And I ask that you keep my body pure, keep my spirit clean, and keep my mind free from unclean thoughts. Thank you for keeping me from giving into temptation, and I thank you for protecting me from compromising my body and my anointing. Amen.

Daily Affirmations

1. I will not compromise.
2. I will not settle for less.
3. I will not put myself in compromosing situations.
4. My body is a temple, and I will keep it clean.
5. I will not conform to the sins of this world.

Personal Prayers

Dear God:

_____

_____

_____

_____

Dear God:

_____

_____

_____

_____

Dear God:

_____

_____

_____

_____

Dear God:

_____

_____

_____

_____

Thank You Notes

Father, I thank you for:

_____

_____

_____

_____

Father, I thank you for:

_____

_____

_____

_____

Father, I thank you for:

_____

_____

_____

_____

Father, I thank you for:

_____

_____

_____

_____

Feeling Afraid

Prayers

D EAR GOD,

I feel so afraid right now, and I don't know what to do. I know your word teaches us not to fear, but at this moment, I feel so afraid about decisions that I've made and situations that I find myself in. And I need to feel your presence so that I won't be afraid anymore. I also ask that you give me wisdom to make the correct decisions for my career, my family, my children, my finances, and the many challenges that I face as a woman every day. Father, I ask that you take away my fears. God, allow me to sleep and rest well with a mind that is free from fear.

Daily Affirmations

1. Fear is only in my mind; I will not be afraid.
2. I speak peace over my mind.
3. Fear is gone, and I will rest peacefully.
4. God has not given me the spirit of fear.
5. God is with me, and I will not be afraid of anything.

Personal Prayers

Dear God:

_____

_____

_____

_____

Dear God:

_____

_____

_____

_____

Dear God:

_____

_____

_____

_____

Dear God:

_____

_____

_____

_____

Thank You Notes

Father, I thank you for:

_____

_____

_____

_____

Father, I thank you for:

_____

_____

_____

_____

Father, I thank you for:

_____

_____

_____

_____

Father, I thank you for:

_____

_____

_____

_____

The Abused

PRAYERS

Dear god,

I come to you today asking that you help me to cope with the abuse that I've experienced in my life. Lord, at times, it is very difficult to talk about these physcial, emotional, sexual, or verbal abuses that I'v been through. So, Father, I come to you in secret asking that you heal me from these scars that were left from the abuse in my life. God, only you know what I really went through, and only you have the prescription for my healing. So heal me, God! I am here crying and praying before you with a heavy heart, please fix me and put me back together again. Lord, make me whole again and rebuild my self-esteem. I ask that you wipe away the guilt and shame that I feel as a result of this abuse. Lord, I need you to help me! And allow me to hold my head up and smile again. I ask these things in your precious name. Thank you for loving me. Amen.

Daily Affirmations

1. I will heal from this abuse.
2. God sees and cares about me.
3. God will take this pain away.
4. Guilt and shame are wiped away from me.
5. I will smile and move forward in God.

Personal Prayers

Dear God:

_____

_____

_____

_____

Dear God:

_____

_____

_____

_____

Dear God:

_____

_____

_____

_____

Dear God:

_____

_____

_____

_____

Thank You Notes

Father, I thank you for:

_____

_____

_____

_____

Father, I thank you for:

_____

_____

_____

_____

Father, I thank you for:

_____

_____

_____

_____

Father, I thank you for:

_____

_____

_____

_____

Grief and Mourning

Prayers

D<small>EAR GOD,</small>

I ask that you heal my grieving heart and soul. Lord, I desperately need you to be with me and comfort me during this time of mourning. This pain seems unbearable at times, and I don't feel like I can make it without my loved ones. I really need you! Please send your angels my way to minister to me during this painful time of need. I miss them so much. Lord, help me to focus on the precious memories that I still have in my heart and mind. Father, I need your strength to get through this hurting time in my life. I also ask that you keep me from turning to drugs, alcohol, or any other self-medicating methods that I think would ease the pain. Father, please help me to hold on and wait on you. Lord, I miss their touch so much. But, God, I ask that you stretch your arms toward me, and hug me as a father holds and comforts his daughter. Father, please wipe away my tears with your soothing hands. I ask these things in your name. Amen.

Daily Affirmations

1. I will focus on the good and precious memories.
2. I will go through the proper steps of grief.
3. I will not self-medicate with alcohol, drugs, etc.
4. I will seek support from family, friends, and support groups.
5. I welcome the peace of God to fill my grieving heart.

Personal Prayers

Dear God:

_____

_____

_____

_____

Dear God:

_____

_____

_____

_____

Dear God:

_____

_____

_____

_____

Dear God:

_____

_____

_____

_____

Thank You Notes

Father, I thank you for:

_____

_____

_____

_____

Father, I thank you for:

_____

_____

_____

_____

Father, I thank you for:

_____

_____

_____

_____

Father, I thank you for:

_____

_____

_____

_____

Suicidal Thoughts

Prayers

Dear god,

This is a desperate plea for you help! I need you! I feel that sometimes the challenges in my life are so heavy, and I don't feel like living anymore. I am so tired, and I don't know what to do. I've been having these thoughts of suicide, and I really need your help. Please rescue me! Please take control of my thoughts and rebuke the powers of darkness from my mind. I need to know that you are right here with me. I really don't want to do this, so please save me right now. Let me feel your presence, and let me know that I have a reason to live! God, I really need you! I need your peace. I choose life. Please, please rescue me!

Daily Affirmations

1. I choose life over death.
2. My life is worth living.
3. I shall live and not die.
4. I will seek professional counseling.
5. I will ask for help from my pastor or church leaders.

Personal Prayers

Dear God:

_____

_____

_____

_____

Dear God:

_____

_____

_____

_____

Dear God:

_____

_____

_____

_____

Dear God:

_____

_____

_____

_____

Thank You Notes

Father, I thank you for:

_____

_____

_____

_____

Father, I thank you for:

_____

_____

_____

_____

Father, I thank you for:

_____

_____

_____

_____

Father, I thank you for:

_____

_____

_____

_____

Strength and Guidance

Prayers

Dᴇᴀʀ ɢᴏᴅ,

I ask that you strengthen my mind as well as my body. Lately, I've been feeling so weak and so tired. I need your strength in order to make it through the challenges that I'm facing. I need your strength and wisdom when making decisions regarding my family, my faith, my relationship, and my life. Please lead and guide me to stay on the path that you have set for me. And if I happen to stray away from your path, please guide me with your light, so I may get back on the path that you have set for me. I thank you for strengthening me, and I thank you for guiding me. Amen.

Daily Affirmations

1. God will lead me in the right path.
2. God will help guide my decisions.
3. God will strengthen my spirit.
4. God will strengthen my mind.
5. God will keep me from falling.

Personal Prayers

Dear God:

_____

_____

_____

_____

Dear God:

_____

_____

_____

_____

Dear God:

_____

_____

_____

_____

Dear God:

_____

_____

_____

_____

Thank You Notes

Father, I thank you for:

_____

_____

_____

_____

Father, I thank you for:

_____

_____

_____

_____

Father, I thank you for:

_____

_____

_____

_____

Father, I thank you for:

_____

_____

_____

_____

Forgiveness

Prayers

DEAR GOD,

I ask that you please forgive me for all of my sins. Forgive me for all the things I've said and done that wasn't pleasing in your sight. Forgive me for the times I may have mistreated others. And forgive me for the many times that I ignored your advice and your warnings. Please forgive me for any sins that I have committed against you, my family, my spouse, my friends, or my children. I ask that you cleanse and forgive me for having a lying spirit, unclean language, lustful thinking, committing fornication, engaging in adultery, or simply grieving your Holy Spirit. For those things and many more, I ask for your forgiveness. Lord, I need you to cleanse me from the crown of my head to the soles of my feet. So today, I kneel down and cling to the rugged cross, and I ask you to wash away my sins and create in me a clean heart and give me a righteous spirit. Amen.

Daily Affirmations

1. I will forgive myself.
2. God will forgive and redeem me.
3. I will forgive others because God has forgiven me.
4. My past has been forgiven, and now I am free.
5. I thank God for his redemption and forgiveness.

Personal Prayers

Dear God:

_____

_____

_____

_____

Dear God:

_____

_____

_____

_____

Dear God:

_____

_____

_____

_____

Dear God:

_____

_____

_____

_____

Thank You Notes

Father, I thank you for:

_____

_____

_____

_____

Father, I thank you for:

_____

_____

_____

_____

Father, I thank you for:

_____

_____

_____

_____

Father, I thank you for:

_____

_____

_____

_____

Lord, Have Mercy

Prayers

D<small>EAR</small> <small>GOD</small>,

I need your grace and mercy. I've said and done some things that I'm not proud of doing, and I need your mercy right now. You word says you provide us with new mercies every single day, and I thank you for caring enough of me to provide your mercy toward me. And I thank you for your extended mercies for the many times I messed up. In Romans 3:23, your Holy Bible clearly states, "All have sinned, and come short of the glory of God" (KJV). So I thank you for having grace and mercy on me. Amen.

Daily Affirmations

1. Lord, have mercy on me.
2. My sins are forgiven.
3. I have God's grace on my life.
4. I thank you for your mercy.
5. I will extend mercy to others.

Personal Prayers

Dear God:

_____

_____

_____

_____

Dear God:

_____

_____

_____

_____

Dear God:

_____

_____

_____

_____

Dear God:

_____

_____

_____

_____

Thank You Notes

Father, I thank you for:

_____

_____

_____

_____

Father, I thank you for:

_____

_____

_____

_____

Father, I thank you for:

_____

_____

_____

_____

Father, I thank you for:

_____

_____

_____

_____

God's Peace

Prayers

DEAR GOD,

I have had so many storms and tragedies in my life, and I desperately need your peace. I need your peace to fall ever so gently on my mind, my body, and my spirit. God, please allow your peace and your Holy Spirit to rest upon my life at this very moment. I ask that you cause the raging seas in my life to become calm and still. Peace be still. Speak peace in the midst of the trials and tribulations that I am facing. I need your peace that passes all understanding to show up in my life. Father, I give my worries, my fears, and burdens over to you. So please allow me to lay down and sleep knowing that your soothing peace is resting on me. I thank you for your peace! Amen.

Daily Affirmations

1. I have peace that passes all understanding.
2. My mind is covered by the peace of God.
3. I have peace in my mind, body, and spirit.
4. I have peace to make it through the trials of life.
5. I will fall asleep and rest in God's peace.

Personal Prayers

Dear God:

_____

_____

_____

_____

Dear God:

_____

_____

_____

_____

Dear God:

_____

_____

_____

_____

Dear God:

_____

_____

_____

_____

Thank You Notes

Father, I thank you for:

_____

_____

_____

_____

Father, I thank you for:

_____

_____

_____

_____

Father, I thank you for:

_____

_____

_____

_____

Father, I thank you for:

_____

_____

_____

_____

Thank You, Lord

Prayers

D<small>EAR GOD</small>,

This humble prayer is just to tell you thank you! Lord, I thank you for all of the miracles and blessings you performed in my life. I thank you for my family, thank you for my children, and I thank you for my life. I give you thanks for letting me know that I'm beautiful and that my life is worth living. God, I thank and praise you for giving me the strength to push through the trials and tribulations of this life. I may not have everything I want, but I thank you that I have everything I need. I thank you for a roof over my head, a comfortable bed to lie down in, food on my table, a car in the driveway, feet to walk with, and clothes on my back. Thank you for helping me to choose life over death. I thank you for not leaving me, and I praise you for not forsaking me. I give you the highest praise for being a father to me, and I especially thank you for caring for me and for embracing me as one of your precious daughters. And, God, I thank you for loving me. Amen.

Call to Salvation

"SEEK YE THE Lord while he may be found, call ye upon him while he is near" (Isaiah 55:6, KJV). I believe this section is the most important portion of this book. I wrote this book to speak to the needs and burdens of women, but I could not conclude without offering a prayer of salvation to those women who don't know God as their Lord and Savior. So to everyone reading the words in this book, if you want a deeper relationship with God and you want to turn away from your sins and give your heart to God, then say this prayer to God and you will be saved:

> Dear Heavenly Father, I ask that you please forgive me for all of my sins. I repent of my sins, and I ask that you save my soul from destruction. I am a sinner, but I want to be saved, so I'm turning away from sin and evil, and I'm looking toward you to save me and to help me be a better person. Father, I want to get to know you more. I want to walk with you, and I want you to walk and talk with me. Lord, please hold my hand as I walk the path that you have set for me. Lord, please cleanse my heart and mind from sins and impurity. Father, I thank you for saving me! Amen.

And, my dear sisters, if you prayed that prayer just now, then you are now saved by God and the angels in heaven are now rejoicing at your decision to serve the Lord. And I am also rejoicing knowing that you have chosen to walk with God. I ask that you find a church or a Bible study group so that you can continue to grow in knowledge by studying the Word of God. And just know that I am smiling and rejoicing with you!

Now, there are going to be challenges in your life, but know that you are not going through those challenges alone. God is standing right there with you, and He will never leave you nor forsake you. May God continue to bless and protect you, and may his face shine upon you and give you peace. I love each of you as my sisters in Christ, and God loves you unconditionally as his precious daughters. Be healed, be encouraged, and don't forget to pray!